Author's Note

Polar bears are a vulnerable and threatened species.

Until well into the 20th century, polar bears were hunted for sport, food, clothing, and traditional crafts. By the 1950s, unregulated hunting for sport and furs was threatening their very survival.

This ended in 1973, with the signing of "The Agreement on the Conservation of Polar Bears," which banned sport and commercial hunting, finally giving legal protection to these bears and their environments.

Today the biggest threat to their survival is climate change. This is because polar bears depend on sea ice to hunt for food, but as the world's temperatures rise, Arctic ice has begun to melt earlier in the summer and freeze later in the autumn. This means that polar bears now have less available food during the summer months. Should a bear already be underweight, the length of time it now has to wait for the ice and its food to return may just be too long.

Polar bears are intelligent, playful, curious creatures. Along with caring for the rest of the natural world, we need to care for these bears and their environments. Only with our commitment to protecting our planet will polar bears be able to truly flourish and multiply in their Arctic homes.

For very special friends: Becks,
Cass, Jess, Lou & Rob, with love

We gratefully acknowledge Geoff York, Senior Director of Conservation at Polar
Bears International, for his time, expertise, and generous commitment to this book.

This book is printed on recycled paper.

www.enchantedlion.com

First edition, published in 2016 by Enchanted Lion Books,
67 West Street, Studio 317A, Brooklyn, NY 11222
Text and Illustrations copyright © 2016 by Jenni Desmond.
www.jennidesmond.com
A CIP record is on file with the Library of Congress. ISBN 978-1-59270-200-8
Printed in China in December 2016 by RR Donnelley Asia Printing Solutions Ltd.
3 5 7 9 10 8 6 4 2

THE POLAR BEAR

JENNI DESMOND

ENCHANTED LION BOOKS

NEW YORK

Once upon a time, a child took a book from the shelf and started to read...

She read that the polar bear is also called a sea bear, and that this huge marine mammal spends most of its life on the ice and snow of the frozen Arctic Ocean. In the spring and autumn, the flexible sea ice can bend and give way under the polar bear's colossal weight. In the summer, there is virtually no ice to hunt across. In winter, the polar bear walks for miles over solid expanses of ice in search of food.

Polar bears live at the northernmost point of the earth, in the Arctic regions of the United States (Alaska), Canada, Greenland, Norway, and Russia. In summer, the Arctic sun never sets. In winter, the sun never rises, and the only light is from the moon, stars, and green glow of the Northern Lights.

Winter temperatures are so low that breath freezes instantly. Harsh winds, blinding snowstorms, and treacherous ice form the environment in which polar bears live for many months. Yet remarkably, they maintain the same body temperature as our own. Big, with heavy limbs, they have two layers of fur, a tough hide, and a thick layer of fat under their skin.

SMALL FURRY EARS

DARK BROWN EYES

BLUE/BLACK TONGUE

42 LONG, SHARP TEETH

BAD BREATH

LONG NECK

LONG, THICK LEGS

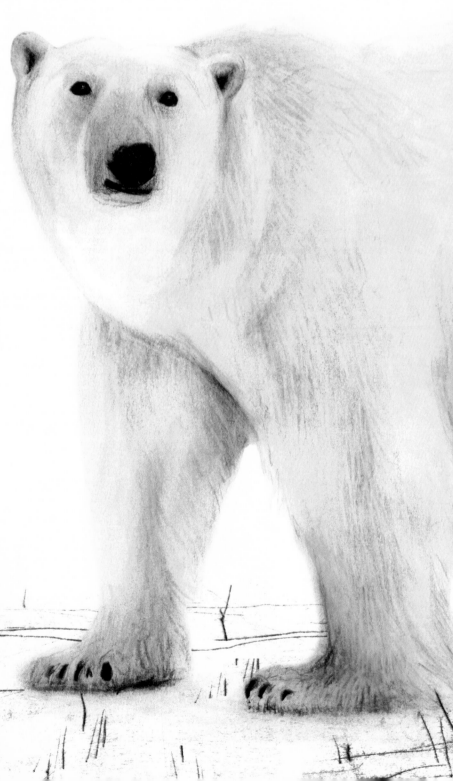

Polar bears evolved to have long necks, so they can keep their heads above water while swimming and reach into holes in the ice for seals. Male polar bears have stronger necks than females, for fighting other bears. Males also have larger bodies, longer teeth, and broader heads.

SHORT TAIL

THEY GROWL, ROAR, CHUFF, HISS, WHIMPER AND PURR

HUGE FEET

Polar bears have huge paws that turn slightly inward. These can be up to 13 inches long, the size of a large dinner plate. While their paws are good for digging and swimming, they also act like snowshoes, spreading out the bear's weight as it moves across deep snow and fragile ice. Should the sea ice begin to bend, a polar bear will crawl on its tummy.

Each paw has five sharp, strong claws and foot pads that are covered with small bumps, much like the surface of a basketball. These claws and pads allow for a strong grip on the ice.

When wet, polar bears shake water and ice out of their fur just like dogs.

The polar bear's fur has two layers: a soft, woolly undercoat and a top layer of water-repellent hairs that are oily, stiff, shiny, see-through, and hollow.

A polar bear looks white in bright sunlight but its coat is really yellow or gray, and its skin is black.

Polar bears are about the same length as two seven-year-old children, top to toe. Males can be nine feet long, while females are usually no more than eight feet.

An adult male might weigh 1,000 pounds, which is around the same weight as 20 seven year olds. Adult females typically weigh half that (500 lbs), unless they are pregnant. Then they can weigh as much as a male.

A polar bear's eyesight is similar to our own, but their eyes have an extra layer that works like a pair of built-in sunglasses. This layer protects their eyes from strong Arctic light and helps them to keep their eyes open underwater.

A polar bear's hearing is also similar to our own, but its sense of smell—its strongest sense—is extraordinary. A bear can smell seals from several miles away and relies on scent to find a mate, detect danger, and locate its cubs. When polar bears stand up on their hind legs, it's so they can smell the air even better.

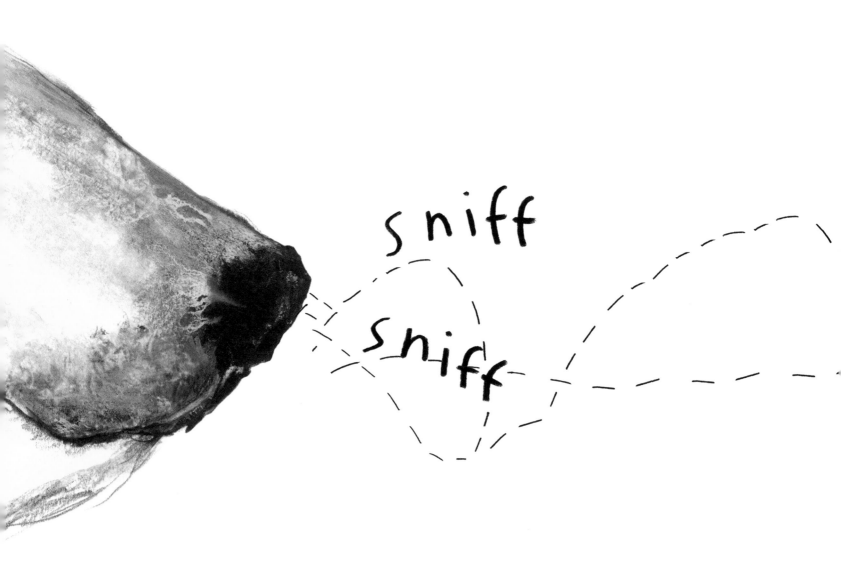

sniff

sniff

In the wild, adult bears usually live for 20-25 years. Solitary creatures, they spend a lot of time alone. Their main reasons for being with others are mating, raising cubs, or feeding upon large food sources, such as beached whale carcasses.

In zoos, where polar bears aren't subject to harsh weather conditions and don't work to find food, they can live into their 40s.

Just as we can know the age of a tree from counting the rings inside its trunk, the rings inside a polar bear's tooth indicate how long it's been alive.

Sniff
Sniff

The best time for polar bears to hunt is in late spring, when
the ice starts to melt and seals can be reached more easily
through the thinner ice. The polar bear's main food is the ringed
seal, but it also eats bearded, harp, and hooded seals, along with the
carcasses of beluga whales, walruses, narwhals, and bowhead whales.

Finding food can be difficult, but polar bears don't have to eat every day.
A single adult seal can satisfy a bear for up to 11 days. Only when summer
arrives and the seals move out into the open water do polar bears largely lose
their food supply. Then, a bear might not eat for three long months, as it waits
for the sea ice to form again.

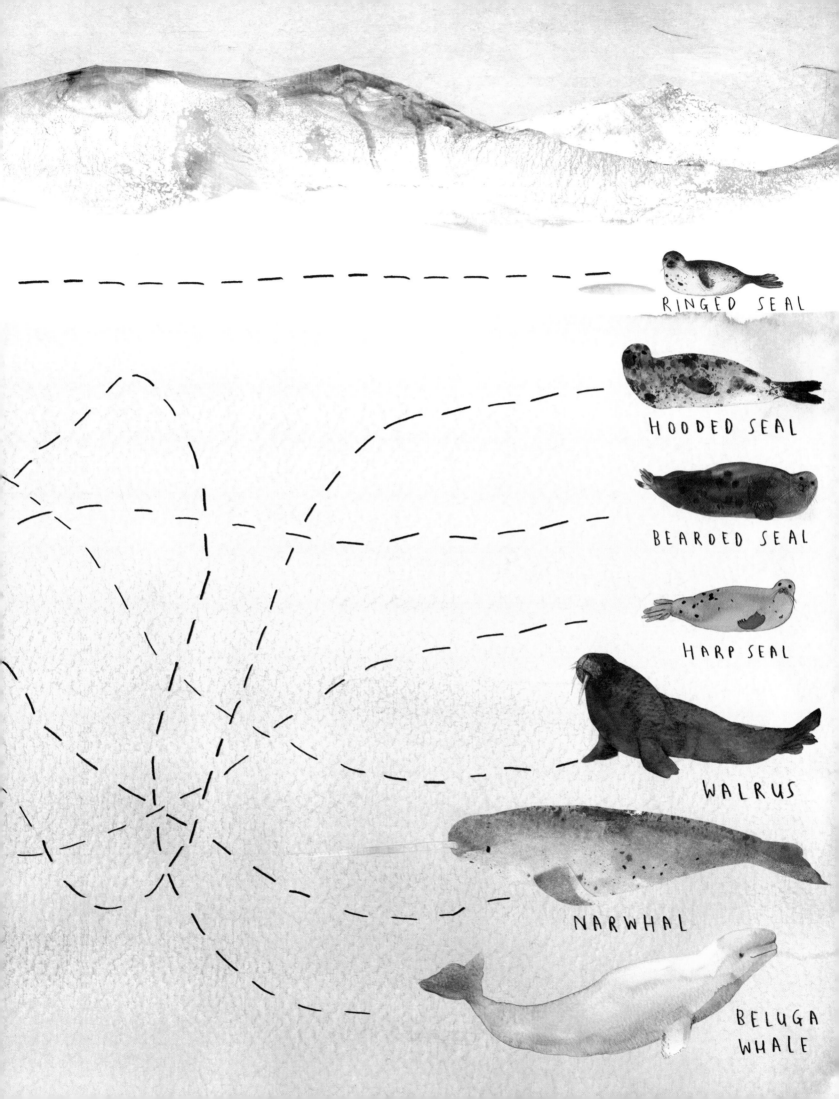

RINGED SEAL

HOODED SEAL

BEARDED SEAL

HARP SEAL

WALRUS

NARWHAL

BELUGA
WHALE

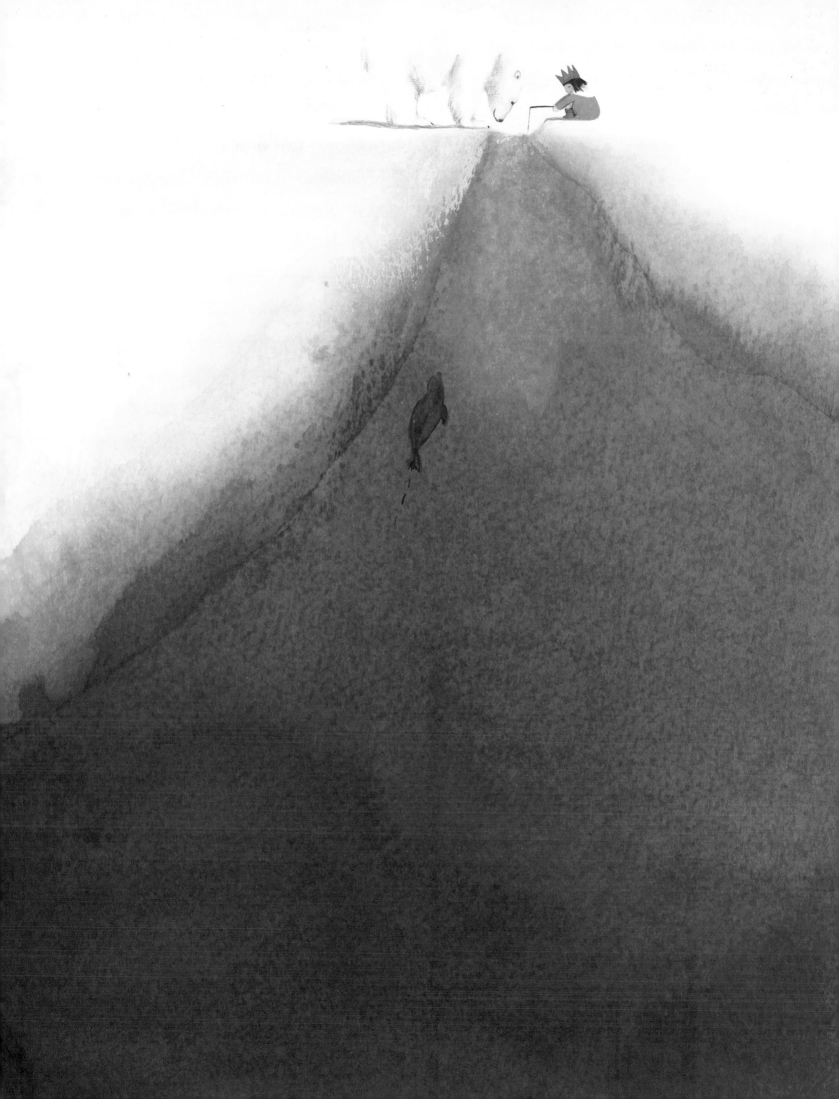

Polar bears have three ways of hunting. The most common is waiting by a hole or at the edge of the ice for a seal to surface. Then the bear will grab the seal with its teeth and pull it onto the ice.

Another is sneaking up on a seal that is already on the ice and then running at full speed to catch it. A polar bear can run faster than the fastest human, but only for a few seconds.

Finally, if a polar bear smells a seal hiding just below the ice in a birthing lair, it will rise up on its hind legs before crashing down through the ice for it.

Seals are wary creatures and faster swimmers than polar bears, so once out in the open water they are difficult to catch. Polar bears kill only one of every 20 seals they hunt. To survive, a polar bear needs to eat around 40 ringed seals a year. Bears always eat the fat and skin first, since those provide the most energy. They also get their water from the seal's fat, since sea ice is too salty to drink.

A polar bear's face is usually stained with blood after eating, but since bears are fussy about cleanliness, they always wash when they have finished. A bear will either wash its paws and nose in a nearby pool or roll around on the ice, rubbing its paws and face in the snow.

Polar bears like to roam on sea ice where there are lots of water channels, cracks, and pools, as these make seals easier to catch. Throughout the year, a bear will stay within an area of ice that is usually hundreds of miles across that is called its home range. Here, ice constantly moves, breaking and shifting with the sea. These sheets of floating ice are called ice floes.

As ice floes break apart, they can move quickly, carrying a bear far from its home range. But since adult bears have an excellent sense of direction and are strong long-distance swimmers, they are able to find their way home. Their fat and the hollow hairs of their coat help them to float, their rounded front paws give them a powerful doggy paddle, and their back legs help them to steer. Polar bears can hold their breath underwater for around two minutes.

In the spring during mating season, a male will follow the scent of a female until he finds her. The bears will then mate, after which the male will often have savage battles with other males to keep her. After two weeks, the male polar bear will depart, scarred from the bloody fighting.

After mating in the spring, a female will only finally become pregnant in the autumn if she has enough stored fat to support a pregnancy. She therefore will spend all spring and summer eating. If she is underweight in the autumn, then she won't become pregnant and will continue to hunt throughout the winter.

Female polar bears dig birthing dens
in sloping snow or peat banks to provide a
warm, sheltered place for their cubs. Once inside,
the female won't eat for many months. Her cubs, usually
born in pairs in December, will stay with her in the den
until spring.

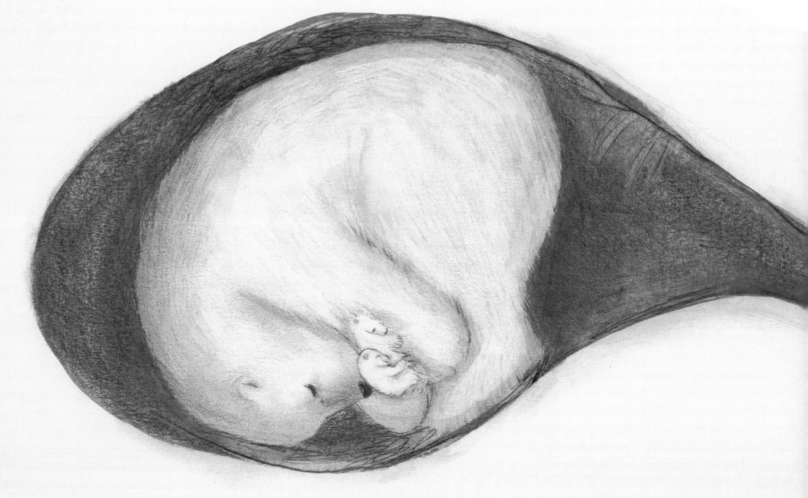

At birth, cubs are pink, the size of a guinea pig,
and covered in soft, fine fur. Their eyes remain
tightly closed for their first month.

Bear cubs feed on their mother's rich, fatty milk and gain weight quickly. After three months, when they are strong enough, the family will travel to the sea ice so the mother can hunt for food.

Cubs spend a lot of time playing—chasing, wrestling, and sliding down small hills. They also watch and copy their mother, who trains them to lie still while she hunts. They sometimes become boisterous all the same and can scare the prey away. Cubs leave their mother after three years, but have yet to become good hunters, so they have to rely on scavenging until their skills improve.

Polar bears do not hibernate. They like to sleep though, and can sleep almost anywhere at any time. Like humans, polar bears sleep in different positions. On warm days, they might stretch out on their back with their feet in the air or lie down on their stomach. On cold, stormy days, they curl up with a paw over their snout for warmth, letting the snow cover them like a blanket.

Most bears sleep a lot when there isn't much food or during bad weather. In areas where the ice melts completely in the summer, a polar bear may spend nearly half its time asleep. Since it's hard to find food without sea ice, it makes sense to save energy and rest.

Just like polar bears, people also curl up in cozy places, perhaps to fall asleep over a favorite book and begin to dream...

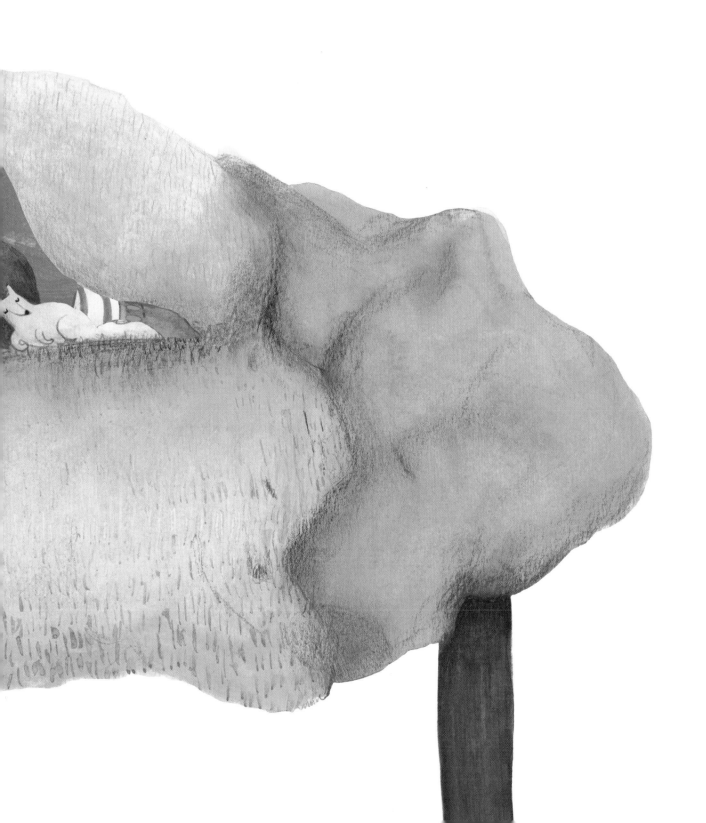